A huge fortune small ads

From the smallest home based business to the large store front you can easily gain more profitable business for pennies on the dollar

William Thomas Lofton Jr

William T. Lofton Jr.

Copyright © 2012 William Thomas Lofton Jr
All rights reserved.
ISBN-13: 978-1539309581

ISBN-10: 1539309584

DEDICATION

Dedicated to all of the businesses out there. You provide something that makes our lives better

CONTENTS

	Acknowledgments	i
1	A huge mistake	8
2	Poor planning	10
3	No advertising plan	12
4	What you can afford	13
5	No advertising budget	14
6	No idea how to advertise	16
7	No customer referral incentive	20
8	Not keeping up with advertising trends	22
9	Not keeping track of results	24
10	Advertising to the wrong customers	26
11	Getting Comfortable	28
12	Getting the message across	31
13	Think about it	34
14	Gimmicks<- Don't be afraid of them	36
15	**The coconut story**	37
16	Affiliations	39
17	**A friend of mine**	41
18	Start right now	45

A HUGE MISTAKE

"WORD OF MOUTH IS THE BEST FORM OF ADVERTISING" THAT PHRASE IS ONE OF THE OLDEST AND MOST WIDELY SPREAD FIBS THAT I'VE EVER HEARD. WHOMEVER STARTED THAT RUMOR HAD NO CLUE ABOUT WHAT IT TAKES TO RUN A SUCCESSFUL BUSINESS. IF YOU DEPEND ON WORD OF MOUTH TO PROMOTE YOUR BUSINESS I PROMISE YOU WILL STARVE! WORD OF MOUTH IS ONLY THE BEST FORM OF CONFIRMATION OF YOUR PRODUCT OR SERVICE AND NOTHING MORE. YES YOU WILL GET BITS AND PIECES OF BUSINESS FROM TIME TO TIME BY WORD OF MOUTH PROMOTION BUT IT WON'T BE NEARLY ENOUGH TO GENERATE A STABLE AND SIGNIFICANT INCOME. JUST ASK ANYONE WHO HAS OWNED A BUSINESS WHETHER PART TIME OR FULL TIME ABOUT HOW WELL WORD OF MOUTH WORKED FOR THEM AND GET READY FOR A LONG AND AWAKENING LESSON MAYBE EVEN A YELLING SESSION AS THEY LET YOU KNOW ABOUT THEIR FRUSTRATION WITH DEPENDING ON PEOPLE TO PROMOTE THEIR BUSINESS.

DON'T GET ME WRONG, YOUR CUSTOMERS MEAN WELL AND ARE GOOD PEOPLE BUT THEIR LIFE IS PRE-OCCUPIED WITH THEIR OWN AFFAIRS SO THEY HAVE VERY LIMITED TIME TO GO OUT AND PROMOTE YOUR BUSINESS FOR YOU. THAT'S YOUR JOB!

CONSIDER THE NUMBER OF TIMES YOU WERE PLEASED WITH A

SERVICE. YOU WERE VERY SATISFIED SO YOU TOLD A FRIEND OR TWO AND MAYBE FROM TIME TO TIME A FRIEND ASKS YOU IF YOU KNOW ANYONE THAT DOES XYZ AND YOU QUICKLY REFER THAT BUSINESS. AND THAT'S ABOUT AS MUCH AS YOU CAN DO FOR THE BUSINESS THAT PROVIDED EXCELLENT SERVICE TO YOU. THE SAME GOES FOR YOUR CUSTOMERS THERE'S ONLY SO MUCH THEY CAN DO TO PROMOTE YOUR BUSINESS.

HERE'S A BIT OF INFORMATION THAT IS TAUGHT IN COLLEGE LEVEL BUSINESS COURSES. IT'S A SCIENTIFIC FACT THAT THE ONLY TIME WE REALLY PUSH A BUSINESS IS WHEN WE WE'RE UNHAPPY WITH THE SERVICE. WE WILL GO OUT OF OUR WAY TO LET ANYONE KNOW ABOUT OUR BAD EXPERIENCE AND WE TRY WITH EVERYTHING WE HAVE TO ENSURE THAT ANYONE WE KNOW OR COME IN CONTACT WITH DOES NOT USE THAT BUSINESS! THIS IS HUMAN NATURE.

William T. Lofton Jr.

POOR PLANNING

I'VE OWNED SEVERAL BUSINESSES DURING MY LIFETIME SOME DID VERY WELL AND SOME DID NOT SO VERY WELL. AND I KNOW QUITE A FEW BUSINESS PEOPLE THAT HAVE SUCCEEDED AND FAILED, AND LET ME SHARE WITH YOU ONE OF THE BIGGEST MISTAKES THAT I SEE IN ANY BUSINESS THAT FAILS IS THAT THEY DO NOT MAKE A PROPER PLAN ON PROMOTION. I MEAN I'VE BEEN DOING THIS SO LONG THAT I CAN TAKE ONE LOOK AT A BUSINESS AND TELL YOU WHETHER IT WILL SUCCEED OR FAIL JUST BY WHAT THEY ARE DOING TO PROMOTE THEMSELVES. I DON'T WANT YOU TO FAIL! I DON'T WANT YOU TO GO THROUGH THE HUNDREDS OF THOUSANDS OF DOLLARS THAT I HAVE GONE THROUGH TO LEARN THESE SIMPLE THINGS THAT I AM GOING TO SHARE WITH YOU. I'VE PUT TOGETHER THIS LIST THAT WILL HELP YOU AVOID THE PITFALLS THAT I HAVE EXPERIENCED AND WITNESSED OVERTIME. THIS LIST WILL WORK FOR THE SMALLEST PART TIME HOME BUSINESS TO THE LARGE CORPORATION. THIS IS THE MAJOR CAUSE OF BUSINESSES FAILING WITHIN THEIR FIRST YEAR OR THREE YEARS AND EVEN AFTER 15 YEARS. PAY ATTENTION TO THIS LIST STUDY IT BURN IT INTO YOUR BRAIN BECAUSE THE LIFE OF YOUR BUSINESS DEPENDS ON IT!

- NO ADVERTISING PLAN
- NO ADVERTISING BUDGET
- NO IDEA HOW TO ADVERTISE
- NO CUSTOMER REFERRAL INCENTIVE
- NOT KEEPING PACE WITH ADVERTISING TRENDS
- NOT KEEPING TRACK OF RESULTS
- ADVERTISING TO THE WRONG CUSTOMERS
- GETTING COMFORTABLE

THERE IT IS, THE CAUSES OF EXTENDED SLOW SPELLS AND DRIBS AND DRABS OF BUSINESS TRICKLING TO YOU! I WILL GO INTO THESE IN DETAIL BECAUSE I WANT YOU TO SUCCEED! WHEN YOU SUCCEED EVERYBODY SUCCEEDS BECAUSE YOU WILL CREATE JOBS AND BOOST YOUR ECONOMY. SO PLEASE CONTINUE TO READ AND STUDY THIS BOOK. I GUARANTEE YOU WILL BENEFIT FROM IT YOU WILL BE AMAZED AT THE RESULTS YOU BEGIN TO GET QUICKLY AND CONSISTENTLY!

William T. Lofton Jr.

NO ADVERTISING PLAN

AN ADVERTISING PLAN IS ESSENTIAL FOR ANY BUSINESS NO MATTER THE SIZE! YOU MUST SIT DOWN AND CREATE AN ADVERTISING PLAN. EVEN IF YOU WRITE IT DOWN ON A NAPKIN (A LOT OF GREAT PLANS HAVE BEEN CREATED THIS WAY) THE MOST IMPORTANT THING IS TO CREATE THIS PLAN AND USE IT.

AN ADVERTISING PLAN IS HOW DO YOU INITIALLY WANT TO ADVERTISE? DOOR HANGERS? FLYERS? THE WEB? HAVE SOMEONE WAVING A SIGN ON THE ROAD? YELLOW PAGES? NEWSPAPER? MAGAZINE? TELEVISION? THERE ARE SO MANY WAYS TO ADVERTISE IN TODAY'S WORLD THAT IT'S MIND BOGGLING. WHAT'S EVEN MORE MIND BOGGLING IS THAT FEW PEOPLE TAKE ADVANTAGE OF THESE OPPORTUNITIES. IF YOU DON'T KNOW WHICH AVENUE TO TAKE PERFORM A WEB SEARCH BY TYPING IN BUSINESS PROMOTION OR ADVERTISING ON YOUR FAVORITE SEARCH ENGINE AND YOU WILL SEE ENOUGH ADVERTISING CHOICES TO FILL UP YOUR EVENING!

ALTHOUGH THERE ARE MANY CHOICES OUT THERE TO PROMOTE YOUR BUSINESS YOU MUST REMEMBER TO ONLY CHOOSE THE ADVERTISING THAT YOU CAN AFFORD FOR AT LEAST THREE TO SIX MONTHS THE LONGER THE BETTER. I WILL GET INTO THIS MORE IN ADVERTISING BUDGET. BUT FOR RIGHT NOW JUST TAKE YOUR TIME AND CHOOSE WHAT SUITS YOU BEST AND

WHAT YOU CAN AFFORD.

AFTER YOU DECIDE WHICH AVENUE OF ADVERTISING YOU PLAN TO USE PLEASE BE SURE TO BUDGET IN IF YOU HAVE TO CHANGE YOUR FORM ADVERTISING AROUND, FOR EXAMPLE WORDING OR AD SIZE. JUST MAKE SURE YOU HAVE ENOUGH TO COVER THIS, IT'S YOUR BUSINESSES LIFE LINE WITHOUT IT YOUR BUSINESS WILL DIE A SLOW DEATH!

AN ADVERTISING PLAN IS JUST THAT, A PLAN ABOUT HOW YOU WILL PROMOTE YOUR BUSINESS. AND NOW WE WILL DISCUSS THE NEXT PART OF YOUR ADVERTISING PLAN…..THE BUDGET!

NO ADVERTISING BUDGET

THIS IS VITAL BUT VERY OFTEN IGNORED. YOU ABSOLUTELY MUST HAVE AN ADVERTISING BUDGET! A BUDGET TO PROMOTE YOUR BUSINESS HAS THE SAME IMPORTANCE AS THE PRODUCT OR SERVICE YOU HAVE TO OFFER! FUNDS MUST BE SET ASIDE TO PROMOTE YOUR BUSINESS AND YOU MUST ADD THE COST OF PROMOTION INTO THE PRODUCT OR SERVICE YOU OFFER. SO THAT YOU CAN SUSTAIN YOUR ADVERTISING THROUGHOUT THE LIFE OF YOUR BUSINESS. WITHOUT A PROPER ADVERTISING BUDGET IN PLACE YOU CAN FIND YOURSELF SPENDING YOUR ADVERTISING DOLLARS WILDLY AND YOU WILL BE OUT OF MONEY BEFORE YOU CAN GET YOUR BUSINESS OFF THE GROUND! SAVE YOURSELF PAIN, HEARTBREAK AND DISAPPOINTMENT SIT DOWN AND COME UP WITH A SOLID BUDGET THAT YOU KNOW YOU CAN AFFORD FOR AT LEAST THREE TO SIX MONTHS. WITHOUT THIS BUDGET YOU ARE HEADED STRAIGHT FOR FAILURE. JUST AS YOU BUDGET FOR SUPPLIES, BUDGET FOR ADVERTISING.

I ALWAYS GET A GOOD LAUGH WHENEVER I SEE A HUGE EXPENSIVE AD IN A NEWSPAPER, MAGAZINE, ON TELEVISION OR IN SOCIAL MEDIA AND VARIOUS OTHER PLACES. THE AD IS A FANTASTIC, HUGE, EYE CATCHING, MESMERIZING COLORFUL, ENTERTAINING WORK OF ART. TOO BAD THEY ONLY CAN AFFORD

TO RUN IT ONCE OR TWICE… IT'S ALL TOO OBVIOUS THOSE FOLKS HAVE A CHUNK OF MONEY…. SORRY MY MISTAKE….. HAD A CHUNK OF MONEY TO SPEND AND ZERO KNOWLEDGE ON HOW ADVERTISING WORKS. YES A BIG FLASHY AD IS NICE BUT IF YOU CAN ONLY AFFORD TO RUN IT ONCE IT WILL NOT BENEFIT YOU. ALWAYS BUDGET FOR LONG TERM! I WILL GO INTO THIS FURTHER LATER IN THE BOOK BUT FOR RIGHT NOW REMEMBER THAT YOU MUST ALWAYS PLAN LONG TERM THERE IS NEVER AN EXCEPTION TO THIS RULE! ALWAYS REMEMBER IS DOESN'T TAKE A FORTUNE TO ADVERTISE. YOU'LL BE SURPRISED HOW MUCH BUSINESS CAN BE DRAWN FROM A SIMPLE SMALL CLASSIFIED AD OR A WELL-PLANNED GIMMICK **(BE SURE TO READ THE COCONUT STORY AND A FRINED OF MINE NEAR THE END OF THE BOOK)**. IT'S A VERY TRUE AND EYE OPENING STORY). OR HOW COST EFFECTIVE WEEKEND FLYER DRIVES CAN BE USING FRIENDS, FAMILY OR PAYING SOMEONE. YOU CAN ALSO HAVE A FLYER INSERTED IN YOUR LOCAL PAPER. THERE ARE NUMEROUS WAYS TO ADVERTISE THAT WON'T MAKE YOU GO INTO DEBT OR FORCE YOU INTO BANKRUPTCY.

William T. Lofton Jr.

NO IDEA HOW TO ADVERTISE

THINK ABOUT THE NUMBER OF TIMES YOU'VE DRIVEN DOWN YOUR NEIGHBORHOOD STREET AND SAW A SMALL SIGN IN THE MEDIAN WITH A PHONE NUMBER ON IT OR THE SIGN SAYS THE NAME OF A BUSINESS ALONG WITH THE NUMBER? CAN YOU RECITE ANY OF THOSE BUSINESS NAMES OR NUMBERS? PROBABLY NOT BECAUSE WE SELDOM PAY ATTENTION TO LITTLE DISTRACTIONS LIKE THAT. BESIDES WERE BUSY DRIVING AND LISTENING TO OUR MUSIC OR RADIO OR TALKING ON THE...... SPEAKERPHONE!

THAT LITTLE SIGN YOU SEE TELLS YOU THAT THE BUSINESS IT REPRESENTS HAS LITTLE TO NO IDEA ON HOW TO PROPERLY PROMOTE ITSELF. OTHERWISE THAT SIGN WOULD NOT BE THERE! OR AT LEAST THEY WOULD'VE HAD A BETTER SIGN STATING A DESCRIPTION OF WHAT THEY'RE OFFERING. AND THAT'S JUST ONE EXAMPLE OF NOT KNOWING HOW TO ADVERTISE. ONCE I SAW WHERE A PERSON SAYS HEY EVERYBODY (SMALL GROUP OF PEOPLE AROUND) I'M STARTING XYZ PLEASE TELL YOUR FRIENDS AND FAMILY! TELL EVERYBODY YOU KNOW!! AND THAT IS THEIR ADVERTISING???? AS I STATED EARLIER NOBODY IS GOING TO PROMOTE YOUR BUSINESS FOR YOU!! ESPECIALLY WITH LITTLE INCENTIVE (MORE ON INCENTIVE SOON). WE'RE BUSY RUNNING

OUR OWN LIVES!

NOW THERE ARE A LOT OF PEOPLE THAT ARE SMART BUT THEY SIMPLY HAVE NO IDEA ON HOW ADVERTISING WORKS. HECK OUR PUBLIC SCHOOLS OFFER BUSINESS CLASSES BUT GOOD LUCK ON FINDING A PUBLIC SCHOOL THAT OFFERS A CLASS ON ADVERTISING BECAUSE YOU WILL NOT FIND ONE! WE ARE NOT TAUGHT THIS VALUABLE SKILL! SO THERE ARE MANY INTELLIGENT PEOPLE THAT START BUSINESSES AND RUN VERY POOR ADVERTISING CAMPAIGNS IF THEY RUN ONE AT ALL BECAUSE THEY HAVE NO IDEA WHAT TO DO. LET ME GIVE YOU SOME EXAMPLES OF POOR BUSINESS PROMOTION THAT IS GUARANTEED TO LEAD TO FAILURE:

1.PUTTING A SMALL ON A ROAD MEDIAN <-FAIL. NOBODY IS PAYING ATTENTION TO THOSE SIGNS. THE ONLY TIME THESE SIGNS WORK IS IF THEIR GIVING YOU DIRECTIONS TO A FUNCTION YOU'RE ATTENDING A HOUSE SHOWING, BIRTHDAY PARTY OR YARD SALE. BECAUSE PEOPLE ALREADY KNOW ABOUT THE FUNCTION AND ARE ACTUALLY SEARCHING FOR THE SIGN. OTHER THAN THAT MOST PEOPLE SEE THEM AS A NUISANCE. IF ANYTHING IT WILL TURN POTENTIAL CUSTOMERS AWAY FROM YOUR BUSINESS.

2.SPENDING ALL OF YOUR ADVERTISING BUDGET ON A PROMOTION THAT WILL ONLY RUN ONCE OR FOR A VERY SHORT PERIOD OF TIME. WE HUMANS ARE BUSY AND IT TAKES TIME

BEFORE AN ADVERTISEMENT SINKS IN, ONE TIME WILL NEVER DO IT. ON AVERAGE WE WILL HAVE TO SEE AN AD AT LEAST THREE TIMES BEFORE WE EVEN CONSIDER THAT BUSINESS. MOST IMPORTANT WE WON'T LOOK AT THAT AD UNLESS IT'S SOMETHING THAT APPEALS TO US OR WE NEED RIGHT AWAY OR IN THE VERY NEAR FUTURE. SO YOU MUST BE OUT THERE CONSTANTLY TO CATCH A CUSTOMER WHEN THE OPPORTUNITY ARISES AND YOU CAN'T DO THAT WITH JUST ONE AD!

3.NOT RESEARCHING YOUR ADVERTISING MEDIUMS. LET ME GIVE YOU A GREAT EXAMPLE OF WHAT I MEAN BY THIS. IF I'M RUNNING A CAR DEALERSHIP WHERE I ONLY SELL CARS PRICED AT $200,000.00 AND HIGHER WHY ON EARTH WOULD I SPEND MONEY RUNNING AN AD IN BARGAIN HUNTERS NEWSPAPER? <- THIS ACTUALLY HAPPENS. OR IF I'M RUNNING A DAY CARE CENTER WHY ON EARTH WOULD I ADVERTISE IN A RACE CAR MAGAZINE?? RESEARCH YOUR MEDIUMS AND MAKE SURE YOU'RE TARGETING THE CORRECT AUDIENCE.

4.FEAR OF ADVERTISING FAILURE. THE ONLY FEAR TO HAVE IS YOU SHOULD BE AFRAID OF NOT ADVERTISING YOUR BUSINESS.

5.THINKING YOU CAN'T AFFORD TO ADVERTISE. YOU CAN'T AFFORD TO NOT ADVERTISE! IF YOU CAN'T ACCEPT THIS FACT YOU'RE NOT READY TO VENTURE INTO BUSINESS FOR YOURSELF. SOME IN THE BUSINESS WORLD REFER TO ADVERTISING AS A NECESSARY EVIL. I REFER TO IT AS LIFEBLOOD. NEVER BE AFRAID

TO CONTACT ANY MEDIUM REGARDING ADVERTISING. MAGAZINES, NEWSPAPERS, WEBSITES NO MATTER HOW LARGE WILL ALWAYS HAVE EXTREMELY REASONABLE AD RATES. YOU WILL BE AMAZED. SO DON'T HESITATE TO CONTACT ANY MEDIUM THAT COMES TO MIND.

William T. Lofton Jr.

NO CUSTOMER REFERRAL INCENTIVE

WE ALL LOVE FREE STUFF IT'S HUMAN NATURE. WANT CUSTOMERS SUPER-FAST? LIKE BY YESTERDAY? WANT YOUR CUSTOMERS TO GO OUT THERE AND PRAISE YOUR BUSINESS AND NEARLY FORCE CUSTOMERS TO COME TO YOU? THEN OFFER INCENTIVES! LIKE I SAID BEFORE WE ARE ALL SO BUSY RUNNING OUR OWN LIVES THAT WE HAVE LITTLE TIME TO PROMOTE SOMEONE ELSE'S BUSINESS. BUT WE ALWAYS HAVE TIME TO GET SOMETHING THAT WILL BENEFIT US. SO GIVE YOUR CUSTOMERS INCENTIVE TO REFER PEOPLE TO YOU. FOR MY CARPET CLEANING BUSINESS I WOULD PROVIDE A FREE ROOM CLEANING FOR EACH CUSTOMER REFERRED TO ME. THE NEXT THING I KNOW I WAS HIRING WORKERS TO KEEP UP BECAUSE ONE PERSON WOULD GO TO HER BEAUTY PARLOR AND TELL HER FRIENDS. ONE PERSON WOULD GO TO THEIR CHURCH AND TELL THE MEMBERS OF THEIR CONGREGATION AND SO ON. BUSINESS BOOMED AND I STILL RAN ADS! I KNEW A CAR DEALER THAT PAID $50 FOR EVERY REFERRAL THAT TURNED INTO A SALE, A LADY IN MY GRANDMOTHER'S CONGREGATION REFERRED PEOPLE TO HIS DEALERSHIP EVERY TIME SHE NEEDED EXTRA CASH! HAVING AN INCENTIVE PROGRAM IS A WIN WIN FOR EVERYONE. YOU GET A NEW CUSTOMER, THEY RECEIVE YOUR QUALITY PRODUCT OR SERVICE AND THE PERSON THAT REFERRED THEM GETS WHATEVER IT IS

YOU PROMISED TO PROVIDE THEM WITH . EVERYBODY IS HAPPY <- THIS IS IMPORTANT IN YOUR REFERRAL PROGRAM. ALWAYS REWARD YOUR REFERRALS!

William T. Lofton Jr.

NOT KEEPING UP WITH ADVERTISING TRENDS

NOT KEEPING UP WITH ADVERTISING TRENDS CAN BE TOXIC TO YOUR BUSINESS. YOU COULD END UP WASTING HUGE AMOUNTS OF MONEY ON ADVERTISING THAT NOBODY PAYS ATTENTION TO ANYMORE. FOR EXAMPLE PAYING FOR AD SPACE ON A PAYPHONE??? NOWADAYS MOST PEOPLE HAVE SMART PHONES AND USE MAJOR SEARCH ENGINES AND OTHER ONLINE AVENUES TO SEARCH FOR SERVICES AND PRODUCTS. THE YELLOW PAGES IS STILL A GOOD PLACE TO BE LISTED IN BECAUSE NOT EVERYONE USES THE WEB TO SEARCH FOR SERVICES BUT BE CAREFUL BECAUSE IT ISN'T THE ADVERTISING POWERHOUSE IT ONCE WAS AND THE SALES PEOPLE ARE AGGRESSIVE AND WILL TRY AND MAKE IT SEEM THAT YOU NEED THEM TO SURVIVE WHICH YOU DON'T. ALSO KEEP IN MIND AS EACH YEAR PASSES WE ARE GETTING CLOSER TO WHERE THE OLDEST POPULATION WE HAVE IS A WEB SAVVY ONE SO DON'T GET COMFORTABLE OR TOO EXCITED ABOUT THE YELLOW PAGES . THERE ARE ALWAYS NEW WAYS TO PROMOTE YOUR BUSINESS POPPING UP, YOU HAVE FACEBOOK <-WHICH I USE, YELP, GROUPON, INSTAGRAM, TWITTER AND TONS OF OTHER ONLINE AVENUES. AND DON'T FORGET

YOUR TRADITIONAL TELEVISION, NEWSPAPER AND MAGAZINES! THESE ARE STILL ADVERTISING POWERHOUSES THAT YOU CAN USE AND BELIEVE IT OR NOT THE PRICING ISN'T AS BAD AS YOU MAY BELIEVE, ADVERTISING SALES PEOPLE THAT WORK FOR MEDIA COMPANIES WILL HELP YOU AND WILL WORK OUT A DEAL FROM TIME TO TIME. THEIR LIVELIHOOD DEPENDS ON YOUR SUCCESS BECAUSE IF YOU HAVE A SUCCESSFUL AD CAMPAIGN WITH THEM YOU WILL COME BACK TO THEM FOR MORE! SO BE SURE TO AT LEAST ASK AROUND AND TALK TO THE REPS! I KNOW A PERSON THAT RUNS A SMALL CLASSIFIED AD IN A FLYING MAGAZINE AND THEY MAKE ENOUGH FROM THAT ONE AD TO COVER A VERY NICE LIFESTYLE.

NOT KEEPING TRACK OF RESULTS

NOW IS THE TIME THAT YOU WILL NEED MICROSOFT'S EXCEL OR SOME OTHER SPREADSHEET PLATFORM SO THAT YOU CAN KEEP TRACK OF YOUR ADVERTISING COSTS AND WHAT KIND OF ROI = RETURN ON INVESTMENT; MEANING HOW MUCH PROFIT ARE YOU MAKING PER CUSTOMER WHEN YOU SUBTRACT THE ADVERTISING DOLLARS SPENT TO ACQUIRE YOUR CUSTOMERS AND CLIENTS.

YOU MUST KEEP TRACK OF WHICH ADS ARE WORKING AND IN WHAT TYPE OF ADVERTISING PLATFORM THEY ARE WORKING IN. BECAUSE YOU WILL FIND THAT AN AD IN ONE PLACE MAY TANK BUT PUT THAT SAME AD SOMEWHERE ELSE AND IT MAY MAKE YOU AN OVERNIGHT MILLIONAIRE! KEEPING TRACK OF ONLINE ADVERTISING HAS BECOME EASIER WITH ANALYTICS WHICH IS SOFTWARE THAT BREAKS DOWN THE TRAFFIC THAT CLICKS ON YOUR AD AND PRESENTED TO YOU IN A NICE AND NEAT PACKAGE , ANALYTICS IS AN AWESOME TOOL BECAUSE IT GIVES YOU EVERY SINGLE DETAIL POSSIBLE ABOUT WHO IS CLICKING ON YOUR ADS IT'S BROKEN DOWN BY WHAT TIME PEOPLE ARE CLICKING WHAT PEAK TIME PEOPLE ARE CLICKING WHAT THEY LIKE HOW MUCH TIME THEY SPEND AT YOUR SITE AND SO ON. RESEARCH ANALYTICS WHEN YOU GET A CHANCE OR

JUST LEAVE IT TO WHOMEVER HOSTS YOUR WEB PAGE…. YOU HAVE ONE RIGHT? I DO (WWW.JUMAXA.COM). AND THEY WILL GIVE YOU A BREAKDOWN OF THE TRAFFIC COMING TO YOUR PAGE EACH MONTH MAKING IT EASY TO HONE YOUR ADVERTISING TO MAXIMIZE YOUR ADVERTISING DOLLARS. ALWAYS BE SURE TO ASK NEW CUSTOMERS HOW THEY FOUND OUT ABOUT YOU. ALSO YOU CAN RUN DIFFERENT INCENTIVES IN EACH AD SO THAT WAY YOU ARE GUARANTEED TO KNOW WHERE YOUR CUSTOMERS CAME FROM, FOR EXAMPLE OFFER FREE PENS WITH EVERY PURCHASE IN ONE ADD AND MAYBE FREE CUP HOLDERS IN ANOTHER SO THAT YOU WILL KNOW WHICH ADVERTISEMENT PULLED WHO.

William T. Lofton Jr.

ADVERTISING TO THE WRONG CUSTOMERS

THE WORST THING YOU CAN DO IS TO ADVERTISE TO THE WRONG PEOPLE. THE ONLY RESULT WILL BE THAT YOU WASTE MONEY AND ENERGY TRYING TO GET SALES THAT JUST AREN'T THERE. FOR EXAMPLE I HAVE A FRIEND WHO STARTED A HEALTH PRODUCTS BUSINESS. HER INVENTORY CONSISTED MOSTLY OF PRODUCTS THAT SHE PURCHASED THROUGH A MULTI-LEVEL MARKETING COMPANY. SHE HAD A STORE FRONT RIGHT IN CHINA TOWN AND SHE HAD A HUGE SIGN ON THE FRONT OF THE STORE AND PAID TO GET A BEAUTIFUL DISPLAY PAINTED ON HER WINDOW THAT PRAISED HER PRODUCTS. SHE EVEN HIRED A PERSON TO PASS OUT BROCHURES TO BY PASSERS. NEEDLESS TO SAY HER BUSINESS FAILED MISERABLY. THE PROBLEM? FIRST, CHINA TOWN IS A TOURIST DESTINATION! PEOPLE DON'T WANT HEALTH STUFF WHILE ON VACAY HELLO! SECOND, WHY WOULD TOURIST BUY STUFF THEY CAN EASILY GET AT HOME? THEY DIDN'T COME TO CHINA TOWN FOR THIS! FINALLY, SHE SPENT ALL THAT TIME AND MONEY WITH A BUSINESS THAT WOULD'VE RUN PERFECTLY OUT OF HER HOME WITH A SMALL CLASSIFIED AD IN A HEALTH MAGAZINE. I ALSO KNOW OF A YOUNG COUPLE THAT TRIED TO SELL SOME SKIN PRODUCTS IN A TOURIST BASED FLEA MARKET AND YOU GUESSED IT, THEY DIDN'T SELL A THING. I'VE KNOWN PEOPLE TO BUY FULLY CUSTOMIZED UTILITY VANS WITH

BEAUTIFUL DISPLAYS PAINTED ON THE SIDES ALONG WITH MUSIC BLARING THROUGH SPEAKERS TRYING TO GET ANYONE IN EARSHOT TO COME PURCHASE NAME BRAND SHOES THEY WERE SELLING….. TOO BAD THAT THE PLACE THEY WERE PARKED WAS A SHOPPING AREA SPECIFICALLY DESIGNED FOR TOURIST! TELL ME THIS, IF YOU EVER GET TO GO TO HAWAII OR IF YOU'VE EVER BEEN TO HAWAII ARE YOU THERE TO BUY TENNIS SHOES THAT YOU CAN GET BACK HOME? BACK HOME FOR A MUCH LOWER PRICE EVEN? HECK NO! YOU'RE THERE TO BUY ONLY STUFF YOU CAN GET IN HAWAII YOU WANT TOURIST STUFF!

William T. Lofton Jr.

GETTING COMFORTABLE

NEVER GET COMFORTABLE WITH HOW YOUR ADVERTISING IS GOING, ALWAYS KEEP UP WITH THE LATEST ADVERTISING TRENDS . THERE'S MANY BUSINESSES THAT GOT COMFORTABLE WITH ONLY ADVERTISING IN THE YELLOW PAGES ASK THEM HOW BUSINESS IS GOING? EVEN IF THEIR BUSINESS IS SURVIVING THEY ARE MISSING OUT ON MASSIVE OPPORTUNITY ON THE WORLD WIDE WEB. I MEAN A COUPLE DECADES AGO THE YELLOW PAGES WAS STILL THE PREMIERE FORM OF ADVERTISING I MEAN THEY COULD NAME THEIR PRICE AND BUSINESSES WOULD FIGHT TO PAY WHATEVER WAS ASKED TO GET THEIR DISPLAY LISTING IN THAT BIG YELLOW BOOK. I MEAN IT WAS SO BAD THAT SOME COMPANIES EVEN RENAMED THEIR BUSINESSES SO THEY COULD HAVE A SHOT AT BEING LISTED IN FRONT OF THE THEIR COMPETITORS. AND THE BUSINESSES THAT HAD THE GREAT SPOTS WITH THE HUGE AND EXPENSIVE LISTINGS SHOWED LARGE DRAWINGS OF WHAT THEIR BUSINESS HAD TO OFFER, I MEAN THEIR YELLOW PAGE DISPLAY WAS AN AD BY ITSELF. AND THOSE PARTICULAR BUSINESSES DID WELL WITH THE YELLOW PAGES FOR DECADES SO THEY GOT COMFORTABLE…….. NOW IT HAS BEEN TWENTY YEARS AND WE HAVE YELP, GROUPON, FACEBOOK, BING AND YAHOO ALONG WITH GOOGLE WHERE YOU SIMPLY TYPE IN WHAT YOU NEED AND A LIST POPS RIGHT UP. WE HAVE POP UP

ADVERTISING. WHERE THEY ALMOST READ OUR MINDS AND SHOW US WHAT WE NEED. AND THOSE THAT ARE STILL FORKING OVER HUGE WASTED MONEY FOR USELESS DISPLAY ADS IN THE YELLOW PAGES ARE BEING LEFT IN THE WIND BY THE BUSINESSES KEEPING UP WITH THE TIMES BY ADVERTISING ONLINE! LIKE I SAID EARLIER THE YELLOW PAGES STILL WORKS BUT IT'S NOTHING LIKE IT WAS 20 OR 30 YEARS AGO AND IT'S STILL FADING. DON'T GET TRAPPED INTO WASTING A FORTUNE ON AN UNNECESSARY AD DISPLAY! FOR WHAT YOU WILL PAY TO HAVE THOSE USELESS DISPLAY ADS A COMPETITOR IS PAYING LESS THAN HALF THAT TO HAVE A WEBSITE AND BE LISTED ON EVERY MAJOR SEARCH ENGINE THERE IS! I MEAN THE BUSINESS LISTED ONLINE WILL POP UP ON ANY SMARTPHONE, NOTEBOOK OR COMPUTER CONNECTED TO THE INTERNET! THIS IS HOW IMPORTANT IT IS TO ALWAYS KEEP UP WITH THE TIMES. KEEP YOUR EAR TO THE GROUND AND ALWAYS BE ON THE LOOKOUT FOR THE NEXT TREND.

WALLA THERE YOU HAVE IT. THE LIST THAT I WANT YOU TO STUDY AND READ AND ABSORB! IF YOU DON'T GET ANYTHING ABOUT BUSINESS STUDY THE ABOVE LIST AND MEMORIZE IT. PASTE IT ALL OVER YOUR HOME UNTIL YOU GET IT IF NECESSARY.

GETTING THE MESSAGE ACROSS

I REALLY WANT YOU TO UNDERSTAND THE IMPORTANCE OF ADVERTISING YOUR BUSINESS SO LET ME GIVE YOU SOME GREAT EXAMPLES. MOVIES AND MUSIC. DO YOU THINK STAR WARS, FIFTY SHADES OF GREY, ELVIS, THE BEATLES, MICHAEL JACKSON AND PRINCE WOULD'VE BEEN A WORLDWIDE SUCCESS WITHOUT THE HUGE PROMOTION BUDGET THE FILM AND MUSIC COMPANIES PROVIDED? ABSOLUTLY NOT!

HECK THERE'S A LONG LIST OF FAMOUS SINGERS THAT DON'T SOUND ANYWHERE NEAR AS GOOD AS SOME OF THE NEIGHBORHOOD SINGERS I'VE HEARD GROWING UP. BUT THE POWER OF ADVERTISING AND PROMOTION PUT THOSE OTHER SINGERS ON THE MAP. WHILE THE NEIGHBORHOOD SINGER IS ONLY ENJOYED BY THE PEOPLE IN THEIR SURROUNDING AREA. THAT IS THE REASON THESE COMPANIES CHARGE THE ARTIST AND WRITERS A PORTION OF THEIR ROYALTIES BECAUSE IT COST THESE CORPORATIONS HUGE FORTUNES TO GET THESE ARTISTS AND PROJECTS OFF THE GROUND! WITHOUT THEIR HUGE INVESTMENT IN ADVERTISING WE WOULD HAVE NEVER ENJOYED WHAT THESE PEOPLE PROVIDED! AGAIN WE'RE NOT TAUGHT ABOUT ADVERTISING AND PROMOTION IN SCHOOL SO WHEN WE HEAR ABOUT THESE COMPANIES CHARGING ARTIST X PERCENT IN FEES AND ROYALTIES WE THINK THE ARTIST IS GETTING ROBBED

BUT IN REALITY IT'S ONLY FAIR BECAUSE THESE COMPANIES HAVE AND STILL DO INVEST MILLIONS UPFRONT TO GET THESE ARTISTS STARTED AND YOU KNOW WHAT? SOMETIMES THESE COMPANIES LOSE MILLIONS BECAUSE OF ARTIST AND FILMS THAT DON'T PAN OUT. I'M JUST TELLING YOU THIS BECAUSE I WANT YOU TO UNDERSTAND THE IMPORTANCE OF ADVERTISING. YOU MUST PUT INTO YOUR ADVERTISING AS MUCH AS YOU PUT INTO THE BUSINESS ITSELF!

LOOK AT COCA COLA AND PEPSI. THEY HAVE A BILLBOARD ON ALMOST EVERY BALL FIELD IN THE COUNTRY! THEY ADVERTISE EVERYWHERE I MEAN THERE ISN'T ONE DAY THAT YOU WILL NOT GO WITHOUT SEEING ONE OF THEIR ADS, EVEN IF YOU LOCK YOURSELF INSIDE YOUR HOUSE YOU WILL STILL SEE THEM SOMEWHERE ON YOUR TELEVISION, ON A PRODUCT IN THE FRIDGE, SOMEWHERE. BUT WHAT THEY DO WORKS BECAUSE WE PURCHASE THESE DRINKS WITHOUT EVEN THINKING TWICE ABOUT IT. I MEAN EVEN AT FUND RAISERS THEY DON'T DARE SELL ANY OTHER BRAND OF COLA BECAUSE WE CUSTOMERS WILL THINK THEY'RE TRYING TO SELL CHEAP STUFF AND WILL NOT SPEND OUR MONEY.

THESE TWO ENORMOUS DRINK COMPANIES KNOW THE POWER OF ADVERTISING! YOU CAN'T GO ONE DAY WITHOUT SEEING THEIR BRAND SOMEWHERE! AND THIS IS HOW YOU MUST BE

WITH YOUR BUSINESS. YOU MUST ALWAYS BE ON THE LOOKOUT FOR COST EFFECTIVE WAYS TO PROMOTE YOUR BUSINESS.

William T. Lofton Jr.

THINK ABOUT IT

THINK OF A COMPANY RIGHT NOW AND AS YOU GO THROUGH YOUR DAY LOOK AND SEE HOW MANY TIMES YOU SEE THAT COMPANIES NAME? AGAIN FOR EXAMPLE COCA COLA, PEPSI OR NIKE. YOU ARE GUARANTEED TO SEE THEIR NAME AT LEAST ONCE A DAY, THAT'S ADVERTISING WHEN YOU THINK OF SODA THEY WANT TO MAKE SURE THEY ARE ON YOUR MIND WHEN YOU DO! EVEN THOUGH THEY ARE THE LARGEST DRINK BRAND IN THE WORLD THEY STILL NEVER LET UP WHEN IT COMES TO ADVERTISING! GET IT? WHATEVER YOUR SERVICE OR PRODUCT IS YOU WANT TO MAKE SURE THAT WHEN PEOPLE WANT OR NEED THAT PARTICULAR PRODUCT OR SERVICE THAT YOUR NAME COMES TO MIND FIRST! THAT'S ADVERTISING! SO REALIZE THAT YOU NEED TO PROMOTE AS MUCH AS POSSIBLE FOR AS LONG AS POSSIBLE, ADVERTISING IS A PART OF YOUR BUSINESS FROM THIS POINT ON.

ALSO, REMEMBER YOU DON'T NEED A HUGE CORPORATE BUDGET TO ADVERTISE A SMALL, SIMPLE AND PROPERLY PLACED CLASSIFIED AD CAN MAKE YOU A HUGE FORTUNE! AND IT HAS FOR MANY!

NEVER, EVER LET UP ON PROMOTING YOUR BUSINESS, LET ME

GIVE YOU A GREAT EXAMPLE. DURING THE 80'S PUMA SHOES WERE ONE OF THE MOST EXPENSIVE STREET SHOES ON THE COMMON MARKET.

AS THEIR INVESTMENT IN ADVERTISING DWINDLED SO DID THE BRAND. IT'S STILL A STRONG BRAND IN AMERICA AND OTHER PARTS OF THE WORLD BUT NOTHING LIKE IT WAS DURING THE 80S I MEAN PEOPLE WERE BEING ROBBED AND KILLED OVER SUEDE PUMAS.

GIMMICKS <- DON'T BE AFRAID OF THEM!

GIMMICKS SOMETHING THAT WILL MAKE YOU STAND OUT FROM THE CROWD. ENTERTAINERS USE GIMMICKS CONSTANTLY BUT THE SMALLER BUSINESSES I FIND ARE SOMETIMES AFRAID TO USE ONE BECAUSE THEY ARE AFRAID OF BEING PORTRAYED IN A BAD WAY. LET ME PROVIDE YOU WITH AN EXTREME EXAMPLE. A STORE THAT ONLY WANTS TO DO BUSINESS WITH PURPLE UNISEXUAL PEOPLE…… BUT GUESS WHAT WILL MORE THAN LIKELY HAPPEN? EVERY NON-PURPLE AND NON-UNISEXUAL PERSON WITHIN A TEN MILE RADIUS WILL PROBABLY COME TO THE STORE TO SHOP JUST TO SPITE THE OWNER……. THAT IS AN EXTREME EXAMPLE, MOST OF THE TIME GIMMICKS ARE FUNNY OR STUNNING. LIKE A BUSINESS THAT HAS BEEN STRONGLY AGAINST SOMETHING FOR 50 YEARS SUDDENLY CHANGES TO BE FOR IT. JUST SIT DOWN AND COME UP WITH AN IDEA THAT WILL SHOCK AND SURPRISE AND CAUSE YOU TO GET ATTENTION. PLEASE KEEP IN MIND THAT MOST BUSINESSES DON'T NEED A GIMMICK BUT IF YOU CAN THINK OF A GOOD ONE FOR YOUR TYPE OF BUSINESS USE IT AND PROMOTE IT! NOW HERE'S THE COCONUT STORY SO YOU CAN GET A GOOD PICTURE IN YOUR HEAD ABOUT HOW WELL A GIMMICK CAN WORK.

THE COCONUT STORY (TRUE STORY)

ON A BEAUTIFUL HAWAIIAN DAY, I SAW A LOCAL HAWAIIAN COME TO THE ALOHA STADIUM'S FLEA MARKET THEY HOST ON WEEKENDS MOSTLY FOR TOURIST. HE PICKED OUT A SMALL GRASSY SPOT AND LAID OUT A SMALL BLUE TARP, HE THEN PROCEEDED TO TAKE HIS SANDALS OFF AND PUT A MACHETE IN HIS MOUTH WHICH DREW TOURISTS ATTENTION (GIMMICK AT WORK HERE FOLKS) NEXT HE CLIMBED THE NEAREST COCONUT TREE AND BEGAN TO HACK AWAY AT THE COCONUTS AND AS THE TOURIST WATCHED IN AMAZEMENT TAKING PHOTOS AND VIDEO THE COCONUTS STARTED TO FALL TO THE GROUND. AFTER HE GOT ABOUT A HALF DOZEN COCONUTS HE CLIMBED DOWN FROM THE TREE GATHERED HIS COCONUTS AND SAT THEM ON HIS LITTLE TARP. HE TRIMMED AND CUT THE COCONUTS IN HALVES AND QUARTERS AND BEGAN TO SELL THEM! FOLKS I PROMISE TEN MINUTES HADN'T PASSED AND HE SOLD OUT AND I SAW HIM WITH A FIST FULL OF MONEY! HE LEFT THE CROWD WANTING MORE! THIS IS ADVERTISING AT ITS BEST! HE WAITED UNTIL THE AREA WAS BUSY AND THEN PERFORMED HIS SHOW AND SOLD OUT IN TEN MINUTES! HE COULD'VE NAMED HIS PRICE AND PEOPLE WOULD'VE STILL BEEN FIGHTING TO GIVE HIM THEIR MONEY FIRST AS THEY ALREADY WERE! I MEAN THIS GUY SNUCK INTO

THE BOWL BECAUSE HE DIDN'T PAY THE FEE TO VEND THERE AND HE ENDED UP MAKING MORE THAN 90% OF THE VENDORS THERE THAT DAY! BEHOLD THIS IS THE POWER OF ADVERTISING TO THE CORRECT CUSTOMER, HOW TO USE A GIMMICK AND HOW COST EFFECTIVE IT CAN BE IF DONE RIGHT ALL IN ONE EXAMPLE. WITH ABOUT $15.00 WORTH OF GEAR THIS MAN WALKED AWAY WITH $280.00 PROFIT IN LESS THAN TEN MINUTES. AND TO THE BEACH HE WENT! NOW IF HE WOULD'VE DONE THE SAME THING AT A SHOPPING AREA THAT CATERS TO LOCALS HE PROBABLY WOULDN'T HAVE SOLD ANYTHING AS LOCALS ARE USED TO THIS AND THIS IS THE NORM FOR THEM. THE LESSON HERE FOLKS IS YOU MUST KNOW WHO YOUR CUSTOMERS ARE AND HOW TO BEST REACH THEM ONCE YOU KNOW THIS YOU CAN DO WELL.

AFFILIATIONS

WHEN I OWNED A CARPET CLEANING COMPANY IN HAWAII I USED A STEAM CLEANING SYSTEM TO CLEAN MY CUSTOMERS CARPET AND FURNITURE. WELL SOMETIMES MY CUSTOMERS WERE PRESSED FOR TIME AND COULD NOT WAIT FOR THE TIME IT TOOK FOR THE CARPETS TO DRY. WELL LUCKILY FOR THEM AND ME I HAD AN AFFILIATION AGREEMENT WITH ANOTHER CARPET AND UPHOLSTERY BUSINESS THAT USED A DRY CLEANING SYSTEM ON THEIR CUSTOMERS FURNITURE AND CARPETS. SO I WOULD REFER MY CUSTOMERS TO THEM AND THEY WOULD DO THE SAME WHEN A STEAM CLEANING SYSTEM WAS THE ONLY WAY TO GET THE JOB DONE. ALWAYS REMEMBER THAT THE BUSINESS COMMUNITY IS ONE BIG COMMUNITY THAT CAN WORK TOGETHER TO HELP EACH OTHER GROW. AS YOU CAN SEE ALTHOUGH OUR TWO BUSINESSES WERE ALMOST THE SAME WE STILL FOUND A WAY TO HELP EACH OTHER. AFFILIATION CAN GET YOU A LOT OF BUSINESS. TRY AND SEE IF YOU CAN GET ANOTHER BUSINESS TO REFER CUSTOMERS TO YOU AND YOU TO THEM. THERE IS A TRUST FACTOR SO ENSURE TO KEEP TRACK OF THE AMOUNT OF BUSINESS IS BEING GENERATED FROM AFFILIATION REFERRALS. THERE WILL ALWAYS BE SOMEONE WILLING TO AFFILIATE, ESPECIALLY BUSINESS THAT HAVE BEEN OPEN FOR A LONG TIME THEY ARE USUALLY VERY

WARM TO AFFILIATION. I RECOMMEND THIS BE THE FIRST PLACE YOU START.

A FRIEND OF MINE (ANOTHER TRUE STORY)

A WONDERFUL EXAMPLE OF HOW WELL ADVERTISING CAN MAKE YOUR BUSINESS LIFE RUN IS ABOUT THE CARPET CLEANER THAT GOT ME STARTED IN BUSINESS. I WILL NEVER FORGET PULLING UP BESIDE HIM IN HIS BLUE TOYOTA TRUCK WITH THE PORTABLE CARPET CLEANING MACHINE ON THE BACK AND HIS MAGNETIC SIGN ON BOTH SIDES OF HIS TRUCK DOORS "CARPET CLEANING $15 PER ROOM 408-XXX-XXXX" HE HAD ON A T SHIRT SHORTS AND TENNIS SHOES A BEARD AND WAS ONE OF THE MOST LAID BACK BUSINESSMEN I'VE EVER MET. HE TOLD ME ABOUT THE PROFIT POTENTIAL OF THE CARPET CLEANING BUSINESS AND THAT THE TWO SIGNS ON HIS TRUCK ALONE BRING IN OVER $2600 PER MONTH IN BUSINESS. WE TALKED FOR A WHILE ABOUT LIFE AND BUSINESS AND I NEVER FORGOT HOW HAPPY HE WAS AND ABOUT HOW MUCH HE ENJOYED HIS FREEDOM AND HOW HE TOLD ME THAT THERE IS ENOUGH BUSINESS OUT THERE FOR EVERYONE YOU JUST GOT TO GO GET IT. THAT HOUR WE TALKED SEEMED LIKE TEN MINUTES AS HE GAVE ME THE MOST VALUABLE LESSON I HAVE EVER LEARNED IN MY LIFE. AT THE TIME I DIDN'T REALIZE HOW VALUABLE AND HOW TO FULLY APPLY WHAT HE TOLD ME BUT AS I GREW AND GOT OLDER IT ALL FINALLY SANK

IN. WELL AFTER OUR MEETING I STARTED A CARPET CLEANING COMPANY, I BOUGHT THE PORTABLE MACHINE, MADE CARDS, BOUGHT RECEIPT BOOKS AND GOT A CELL PHONE LINE FOR THE BUSINESS. I DIDN'T BUY THE DOOR SIGN YET BUT I PASSED OUT CARDS TO FRIENDS AND GOT A COUPLE PIECES OF BUSINESS. BUT BARELY ANYTHING TO FILL UP THE GAS TANK. THEN I REMEMBERED WHAT HE SAID ABOUT HIS DOOR MAGNETS THAT THEY WERE HIS INSTANT AND CONSTANT ADVERTISING. AND WOULDN'T YOU KNOW IT I WAS WALKING INTO THE GROCERY STORE AND SAW A STACK OF PENNY SAVER NEWSPAPERS, IT ALL DAWNED ON ME AT ONE TIME. YES WORD OF MOUTH WAS GETTING ME CRUMBS. BUT TO GET THE REAL BUSINESS AND REAL INCOME I NEEDED TO ADVERTISE. SO I PICKED UP THE PENNY SAVER TO FIND OUT HOW TO CALL AND GET MY AD STARTED AND WOULDN'T YOU KNOW IT. AS SOON AS I TURNED TO THE SECOND PAGE THERE WAS THAT CARPET CLEANERS AD RIGHT IN THE CENTER SO IT COULDN'T BE MISSED.

Carpet Cleaning

$15.00 per room

408-xxx-xxxx

AFTER TALKING TO THE PENNY SAVER FOLKS I CREATED MY OWN AD AND THE DAY AFTER THE FIRST RUN I WAS GETTING CALLS!!! I WAS GETTING ACTUAL CUSTOMERS!!!

WELL AFTER A FEW YEARS IN THE AREA WE LIVED I SAW A RED TRUCK WITH THAT SAME MAGNETIC SIGN ON BOTH THEIR DOORS THAT HAD THE SAME PHONE NUMBER AS THAT GENTLEMAN THAT I HAD MET. THERE WERE TWO YOUNG MEN UNLOADING THE TRUCK ABOUT TO GO INTO A HOME TO CLEAN THE CARPET, I TALKED TO THEM AND WOULDN'T YOU KNOW IT. THEY WERE HIS EMPLOYEES. THEY WENT ON TO TELL ME THAT THE OWNER STAYS AT HOME RUNS THE BUSINESS OUT OF HIS HOME AND HAS A PRETTY SECRETARY ANSWERING HIS PHONE AND MAKING APPOINTMENTS! I WAS AMAZED AT HOW MUCH HIS BUSINESS HAD GROWN! BUT THEN I REMEMBERED SOMETHING HE SAID THAT IT TOOK HIM A FEW TRIES WITH HIS AD TO SEE WHAT WORKED BEST BUT AFTER THAT EVERYTHING WAS AUTO-PILOT! AND WHAT AN AUTO-PILOT! I MEAN THE AD DREW IN THE CUSTOMERS SO WELL THAT HE WAS ABLE TO SIT BACK AND ENJOY THE BUSINESS AND LIVE HIS LIFE! THAT SIMPLE "CARPET CLEANING $15.00 PER ROOM" AD WAS AN INCOME POWERHOUSE! I'M SHARING THIS WITH YOU BECAUSE I WANT YOU TO UNDERSTAND THE POWER OF ADVERTISING AND HOW IT CAN MAKE YOUR BUSINESS A SUCCESS BEYOND YOUR WILDEST DREAMS AND YOU WILL BE ABLE TO HAVE THE LIFE YOU'VE ALWAYS WANTED AND MORE ALL WHILE

YOU ENJOY WHAT YOU DO! ALL WITHOUT COSTING YOU A FORTUNE. ADVERTISE! ADVERTISE! ADVERTISE!

I WENT TO GO VISIT MY OLD FRIEND AND SEE HOW HE WAS DOING (I REALLY WANTED TO SEE IF WHAT HIS WORKERS WERE TELLING ME WAS TRUE) AND WHAT DO I KNOW IT WAS ALL TRUE, THE RECEPTIONIST, HIM SITTING AT HOME ENJOYING LIFE. HE WELCOMED ME WITH OPEN ARMS AND TOLD ME ALL ABOUT IT. HE TOLD ME HOW THAT ONE AD WAS GENERATING MORE INCOME THAN HE EVER THOUGHT IT WOULD AND NOW ALL HE DOES IS RUN A FEW ADS IN LOCAL NEWSPAPERS , THE CUSTOMERS CALL AND THE INCOME ROLLS IN. EVERYTHING RUNS ON AUTO PILOT! HE SHARED ALL OF THIS VALUABLE INFORMATION WITH ME BECAUSE AS HE TOLD ME TIME AND TIME AGAIN THAT THERE IS ENOUGH BUSINESS FOR EVERYONE AND THAT NOT EVERYONE WILL GET IT. AND DARN IF HE ISN'T RIGHT STILL TODAY BECAUSE THERE ARE MANY BUSINESSES OUT THERE THAT WE WILL NEVER HEAR ABOUT BECAUSE THEY FAIL TO ADVERTISE!

LET ME ADD SOMETHING HERE KEEP IN MIND THAT IT TOOK HIM A FEW TRIES BEFORE HE FOUND AN AD THAT WORKED FOR HIM. I WENT THROUGH THE SAME TRIAL AND ERROR STAGE UNTIL I FOUND AN EFFECTIVE AD FOR MY VENTURES. ALWAYS TRY MULTIPLE ADS ON DIFFERENT PLATFORMS BECAUSE THAT IS THE

BEST WAY TO FIND OUT WHAT WORKS AND WHAT DOESN'T AND WHAT I'VE FOUND TO BE TRUE IS THAT SIMPLE WORKS IN MOST CASES (REMEMBER THE GUY WITH THE COCONUTS STORY!) AN ADS ONLY PURPOSE IS TO DRAW CUSTOMERS AND POTENTIAL CLIENTS TO YOU SO THAT YOU CAN WOW THEM WITH WHAT YOU HAVE TO OFFER.

START RIGHT NOW

THERE IS NO BETTER TIME THAN THE PRESENT. START NOW WITH A SMALL AD IN YOUR LOCAL NEWSPAPER OR ONLINE. THE IMPORTANT THING IS TO GET STARTED AND TO TRACK YOUR RESULTS AND CHANGE THINGS UP WHENEVER YOU NEED TO. REMEMBER DON'T HESITATE TO TRY AN AD A DIFFERENT WAY AND TRY MANY ADS BECAUSE ALWAYS REMEMBER THAT WHAT YOU THINK WON'T WORK MAY MAKE YOU AN OVERNIGHT MILLIONAIRE!

Contact me

Any questions feel free to contact me via my website www.jumaxa.com OR simply email me @ jumana@jumaxa.com

www.ingramcontent.com/pod-product-compliance
Lightning Source LLC
Chambersburg PA
CBHW070416190526
45169CB00003B/1284